ZZB

Entanglements

Jack Mayer

Proverse Hong Kong

2022

Note on the cover image (CMS Higgs-event.jpg)

An example of simulated data modeled for the Compact Muon Solenoid (CMS) particle detector on the Large Hadron Collider (LHC) at CERN, the European organization for nuclear research. Here, following a collision of two protons, a Higgs boson is produced which decays into two jets of hadrons (composite subatomic particles, each made of two or more quarks) and two electrons. The lines represent the possible paths of particles produced by the proton-proton collision in the detector. The energy these particles deposit is also shown.

Entanglement occurs at every level of existence. Life is entangled. **ENTANGLEMENTS: PHYSICS, LOVE, AND WILDERNESS DREAMS**, Jack Mayer's second poetry collection, is a poetic mélange about relationships, from sub-atomic particles to our human family; the ties that bind. Mayer, a pediatrician, poet, and hiker, explores the metaphysics of cosmology and that particularly intense entanglement, love. At the macroscopic level, Mayer's doctor poems, inspired by his pediatric practice in rural Northern Vermont, take the reader into the heart and soul of a healer inspired to find meaning in his patients' often difficult lives. Unique connections are unearthed. As a wilderness hiker and canoeist, Mayer has experienced the healing power of wilderness; the mystery of belonging to wilderness, of independence and interdependence. His wilderness poems carry us into his beloved Green Mountains on Vermont's Long Trail. On solo hikes he composes poems, then copies his first draft into the nearest shelter's logbook under his trail name, "Mountain Poet." A durable thread connects these musings on relationships—our fundamental connections. Our quest for meaning depends on relationships, the matrix within which we endeavor to understand. We are entangled.

JACK MAYER is a Vermont writer and retired pediatrician. He was an **anti-Vietnam** war activist in the '60s and was arrested at a demonstration in Chicago in 1969. His legal case, argued before the U.S. Supreme Court (Mayer vs. City of Chicago, 1971), established the right of indigents to have court costs paid by the state. (By the time he was in medical school he had college and medical school debts. His only valuable possessions were his microscope and textbooks. In a *New York Times* article about his trial, the Chicago judge was quoted as expressing his surprise that in America a medical student could be judged an indigent.) In 1976 Dr Mayer established the first pediatric practice in Vermont's Eastern Franklin County on the Canadian border, where he began writing about his practice and hiking Vermont's Long Trail. In the '80s Mayer was an anti-nuclear activist and New England delegate to **Physicians for Social Responsibility**. Dr Mayer was a National Cancer Institute Fellow at **Columbia University,** researching the molecular biology of cancer (1987-1991). He established **Rainbow Pediatrics** in Middlebury, Vermont, in 1991 and retired from his practice in 2021. He was an Instructor in Pediatrics at the **University of Vermont School of Medicine** and a pre-med mentor at **Middlebury College**. Mayer was a participant at the **Bread Loaf Writers' Conference** in 2003 and 2005 (fiction) and 2008 (poetry). His first non-fiction book is *Life In A Jar: The Irena Sendler Project*. His *Before The Court Of Heaven* (2015)—historical fiction about the rise of the Third Reich—has won several awards. Mayer's first poetry collection, *Poems From the Wilderness* (Proverse 2019) won the International Proverse Prize 2019.

ENTANGLEMENTS
Physics, Love,
and Wilderness Dreams

Jack Mayer

Author of *Poems from the Wilderness*,
Winner of the 2019 Proverse Prize

Proverse Hong Kong

Entanglements:
Physics, love, and wilderness dreams
By Jack Mayer
First published in Hong Kong
by Proverse Hong Kong,
under sole and exclusive right and licence,
17 November 2022
Paperback: ISBN 13: 978-988-8492-66-4
E-book: ISBN 13: 978-988-8492-67-1

Distribution (Hong Kong and worldwide)
The Chinese University of Hong Kong Press,
The Chinese University of Hong Kong,
Shatin, New Territories, Hong Kong SAR.
Email: cup@cuhk.edu.hk; Web: www.cup.cuhk.edu.hk
Distribution (United Kingdom): Stephen Inman, Worcester, UK.
Enquiries to Proverse Hong Kong
P.O. Box 259, Tung Chung Post Office,
Lantau, NT, Hong Kong SAR, China.
Email: proverse@netvigator.com;
Web: www.proversepublishing.com

The right of Jack Mayer to be identified as the author of this work
has been asserted by him in accordance with
the Copyright, Designs and Patents Act 1988.

Cover image: Lucas Taylor / CERN, CC BY-SA 3.0
<https://creativecommons.org/licenses/by-sa/3.0>, via Wikimedia Commons

British Library Cataloguing in Publication Data
A catalogue record for the first paperback edition
is available from the British Library

Acknowledgments

I owe a deep debt of gratitude to my editor, Susan Jefts, for her thoughtful reading, commentary, and edits. Neither of us are physicists, yet Susan understands, on a metaphysical level, the implications of quantum theory for our quotidian lives. A gifted poet in her own right, she has helped me shape these musings on relationships and physics into, hopefully, an eloquent whole. Susan intuitively understands the spectrum of human efforts to bring the natural, relational, and subatomic worlds into a coherent focus that informs, challenges, and delights. She has helped shape my poetry into a symphonic whole, always mindful of the reader's sensibility and grasp

Thank you, Gillian Bickley, editor of Proverse Hong Kong, who has also been a careful, vigilant, and prudent editor and shepherd of this collection. I could not ask for a more generous and talented publisher. Any errors which may remain are of course mine alone.

Boundless thanks to my first and last reader, my wife Chip, who has been on this journey with me from wilderness to quarks and black holes with her well-tuned ear, her acumen, sense, and good humor. She is my stalwart supporter and inspiration.

As a physician, I am grateful and honored to express profound appreciation for my young patients and their families who have taught me how to be a compassionate healer in a troubled world. They have been my teachers.

Rich Wolfson **is** a physicist. He is an Emeritus Professor of Physics at Middlebury College. I am so grateful for his review of the manuscript and assessment of the physics. I seem to have gotten it mostly right. Thank you, Rich.

Though I compose these poems alone, in the solitude and fertility of wilderness, they are nothing if not reflections of my panoramic view of the fragile and compelling vistas of what it means to be human.

Ultimately, we only exist because of our entanglements.

Previous Publication Acknowledgements

'Anatomicus Anomalous (or Popliteal Goes the Weasel)' was first published in, *Journal of the American Medical Association*, Vol. 312, No. 22, Dec. 10, 2014. Reprinted by permission.

For my wife, Chip, with deep gratitude for our singular entanglement.

You and I, tender and turgid
green scallion shoots,
luminous, not yet sautéed.

It was the old world.
We were fresh and hot,
gazing at each other
like chocolate in anticipation
of melting.

—from 'Kitchen Hippie', *Entanglements*.

"Reality is this web of interactions."
—Carlo Rovelli
Professor of Physics,
Centre de Physique Théorique de Luminy,
Aix-Marseille University, France.

ENTANGLEMENTS

Physics, love
and wilderness dreams

by Jack Mayer

Author's Note

As a husband, father, friend, musician, and primary care pediatrician, I have learned the importance and mystery of relationships, interdependence, and interconnectedness. As an avid hiker and canoeist, I treasure these qualities in the natural world.

I am fascinated by the metaphysics of physics and the mystery and intrigue of sub-atomic relationships. Each in our own way, we test, poke, and prod our perceived world, probing what is for now unreachable, incomprehensible. We weave complex mathematical theories to explain our cosmos – a secular faith and devotion. As we consider the interactions of sub-atomic particles, approach the frontiers of understanding, relationships emerge. Particles interact, often at staggering distances that beggar our imaginations and suggest the boundaries of science.

We live on the crust of our Earth, the skin of a rocky planet, a dust mote in our galaxy. Day to day living consumes most of our conscious preoccupation with our perceptions of the universe and our being. Every living thing exists in relationship with every other. Even our sense of time is conditional on our relative point of view – on relationship. You and I have a "history" because we believe in what Einstein called the "stubbornly persistent illusion of time." And perhaps 95% of the universe is "dark matter" and "dark energy," about which we know almost nothing, except that it holds us together. Interconnection.

Whether or not there is a point to our existence, and whatever that point might be, we nevertheless strive for elegance, perfection, beauty, and contentment. Relationships seem to be the matrix in which we endeavor to understand. We are entangled.

As a young pediatrician in rural Vermont on the Canadian border, I learned about connection and relationships from my patients. Most profound for me was my weekly house call with the family of a newborn, Jade, with a terminal disease, who lived for six months, during which she received an abundance of love and care. My experience with Jade and her family inspired me to continue writing poems about my practice. This has been the "macro" world of my poetry.

There is also a "micro" world, grounded in Cosmology, in the fundamental laws and theories of physics, the very boundaries of existence, and in the quantum world of particles: quarks, Higgs bosons, muons, neutrinos, and those yet to be discovered. Each is bounteous with metaphor and wonder; another world of connection and relationship. In the world of quantum physics, "entanglement" occurs when two particles are in relation to each other, and actions performed on one of the particles effects the other, simultaneously, no matter the distance between them. They could be on opposite sides of the universe.

Quantum entanglement is a physical phenomenon that occurs when subatomic particles interact in such a manner that each quantum state, each probability space of each particle, can be described only in relation to the state of the others, even when the particles are separated by huge distances. It's all about relationships.

Entanglement occurs at every level of existence. Life is entangled. As we delve deeper and appreciate our biological and physical world on ever smaller scales, we discover entanglements everywhere. The secrets of growth and community, of single cells becoming multi-cellular, and finally becoming us, lie in relationships. The secrets of light, gravity, electromagnetism, strong and weak forces, involve relationships – quantum entanglement.

Uncertainty is all we can be certain of. A flower vase is a probability space of quanta related to me and other quanta. The flowers are temporary improbabilities, as are we. I experience beauty, elegance, the unimaginable and the ineffable.

In the quantum world of physics, the Merlins of our cosmology had already seen (mathematically) entanglements 10^{-35} seconds after the Big Bang. At our limits of observation and comprehension, we begin to understand entanglements between elementary particles – quarks, muons, neutrinos, Higgs bosons, etc. Some day we might even "see" the vibrating strings that underlie elementary particles and understand an 11-dimensional universe.

We are entangled from birth to death and beyond. How we interact is the foundation of culture, history, religion, and, most fundamentally of all, love.

My poems consider the various entanglements of which we are conscious. What we call "love" is a particularly intense entanglement – one that flaunts uncertainty and marinates in hope and beauty. Dreams are stories our unconscious tells, unadulterated by boundaries. We are indeed the subatomic particles of history, and we try to make sense of it all by considering interactions – relationships.

What we perceive is ephemeral – love, particles, dreams. Yet, the Laws of Thermodynamics reassure us that nothing is destroyed – only changes form. And everything tends to disorder. We can forgive and be forgiven.

I hope you will be inspired, delighted, and surprised by my poetic musings upon our connections. The closer we observe, the more we are drawn into the roiling world of entanglement on every level of our elementary understanding.

DOCTOR POEMS

On the Border

Jade
18 August 1983 to 11 February 1984

1) One month (21 September 1983)

"It's a very rare problem."
The geneticist at the medical center
seems pleased with his diagnosis,
eager to teach a young physician
alone on the Canadian border.
"Pena-Shokier, Type I.
Genetics that would wilt Mendel's peas."
Pena-Shokier, Type I.
I think of Native Americans
each time I write
Jade's lethal diagnosis.
The one time you saw the geneticist,
he said with cruel, clairvoyant authority,
"Jade will forget to breathe one day."

A tiny blue tube,
punched through Jade's neck
gurgles and coos.
Black searching eyes animate
her swollen doll's face,
cheeks shiny like porcelain.
Though only a month old,
you tell me she already looks for you,
searches for your voice.

Pam, I see your face in Jade's,
though she has multiple deformities.
The familial mirror is cracked, not shattered.
"I'm up a lot with her at night," you say.
"Everybody tells me to sleep,
but Jade won't be here in six months."

You said it matter-of-factly.
"Then I'll have time to sleep,
but I think I'll always be tired."

Jade did forget to breathe.
The alarm screamed,
not a false alarm this time.
You crossed your linoleum floor
on sure feet,
suctioned the baby-blue tube,
like the Home Health Nurse showed you,
and kept Jade here a bit longer.
You seemed to know exactly
what you were doing.
"I was nervous," you confess,
after I tell you that you are a hero.

2) Five Weeks (23 September 1983)

The grade is steep off Vermont 105
down to your first floor apartment
in a once grand house,
in a once grand town
that the railroad and prosperity left behind.
I feel weightless, cresting the roller-coaster hill.
For a moment of Newtonian indecision
my car balances, tips down
and I fear the fall.
This hill will be a son-of-a-bitch
when it snows next month.

Jade's black hair, lustrous
with synchronized curls,
reflects a healthy glow
from the bare bulb in your bedroom.
Jade sucks her lower lip easily

because her jaw is unnaturally small.
She has a wide-eyed restless gaze.
You tell me she sees everything,
she watches your face.
I think she is blind.
But your faith is so sweet
that I will keep my bitter fruit
from your table a bit longer.
"Please check her vagina.
It was red when I gave her a bath.
She hates her bath."
I think you forget
in Jade's tears and fussing
that she will not be
your messenger of immortality,
that her vagina will never be
inflamed in that way,
only present
to painfully remind you.

3) Six Weeks (30 September 1983)

Indian summer burns red and yellow.
Winter lurks in the Cold Hollow Mountains.
Soon every child in Franklin County will be sick.
You were still in your pajamas
when I came to the house.
Does it mean you are finally sleeping?
You smile and I wonder
about the heart needle
that keeps you awake.
"The doctors (always nameless)
want more tests.
Nothing that will hurt, so they say."
But you are past their suspect comfort.
"They think she has seizures,

but she's so content.
Look at her, Dr. Jack,
no pain, no seizures."
Your eyes catch fire.
"No son-of-a-bitch doctor's
gonna study my Jade.
I know their game.
Tests, then medicine to quiet her down,
to make her sleep,
to take her away.
I only want Nurse Martha to come.
That other one, Corinne,
I'll punch out her lights
if she comes back.
Only Martha. And you. No one else."
A dark shadow stirs
in the queen-size bed beside Jade's crib.
Jade's father in twilight sleep.
 "Here's your coffee, Dr. Jack.
The way you like it,
strong – milk, no sugar."
She gives me a mug from Disney.
"When Dick suctions her tube
I swear she knows to hold still.
In her bath she kicks like a frog and screams.
But when Dick sucks out her tube
She lies as still as –
as can be."

I ask how often you doubt
that she could possibly have
Pena-Shokier type I Syndrome.
"Yeah. Sometimes."
Your eyes shine.
I'm so sorry, Pam.
I'm only the messenger.

I only come once a week
then leave you to hide and seek
among your fantasies,
desires, longing, and doubts.
"She's growing, developing.
Watch this, Dr. Jack.
Watch what she does
when I turn on the suction.
She really knows."
I cannot see what you see
as the churning, gurgling motor
fills your dark bedroom
with its sucking song.
"She never does it when someone watches."

Mandy will be seven next week.
Yesterday she watched her sister
turn "blue as a plum."
"Why can't you fix her?" she asks me.
Mandy's eyes, like Jade's, are dark and large.
You knew you had to tell her
and this is what you said.
"Jade will die one of these days.
She'll go to heaven and someday,
we'll all be together,
in heaven, a family again."
Another cigarette, brief respite.
"You said it was the right thing to say."
Smoke hangs like cumulus under the ceiling.
"You know what Mandy said?
After all that?
She said, 'But Jade will be a teenager then.'
Mandy don't ask much.
But she watches. She sees everything."
Before I even considered
that you might need an embrace,

my arm is around your shoulder.

4) Seven Weeks (6 October 1983)

Your sister carries a dead baby
in her womb.
She was to be born this week.
Its heart just stopped.
No warning, no reason.
You called the same funeral home
to make arrangements for Jade.
When you weep
your mascara smudges and runs.
Ever so slowly
your flesh turns darker.

5) Two Months (21 October 1983)

You are sweeping your linoleum floor
when I come in, early.
Dick is still asleep,
snoring under a dark brown quilt.
"He had the late shift," you whisper.
"We split the night –
8 to1:30 and 1:30 to 7.
I hate it.
Last week, after you left,
I started to itch all over."
Even your skin weeps.
If she "goes" when you're asleep
what will you do?

The ashtray is full
on your coffee table.
The MIDNIGHT ENQUIRER
open to page five, screams

TERMINAL CHILD LIVES
DESPITE DOCTORS' PREDICTIONS.
A loving mother
embraces her son who has defied death.
I know you still pretend
that one day Jade will carry her lunchbox
out this door and return a few hours later.

6) Nine Weeks (24 October 1983)

Jade's grandmother and great uncle hover
like the Burghers of the doomed city of Calais,
keeping vigil with you, with your sleeplessness.
Today you tell me of her seizures,
though you didn't know to name them.
No lightning spasms. No.
Jade's brain is gentle in defect.
She turns a ruddy colour,
the whites of her eyes redden,
she stiffens ever so slightly.
The first time it lasted four hours.
You thought you would lose her
but you did not call.
I suppose that means you know
that Jade's death comes creeping,
inexorably, like winter twilight.

7) 5 Months (18 January 1984)

"She always gets sick on her birthday."
It is not a complaint.
Your eyes mist over like clear pools.
A timeless sigh feather-falls
onto Jade asleep in your lap.
Jade does little more than she did
five months ago,

yet you see temperament, personality.
You teach me how to recognize each
in her swollen moon face.
Her new crib is too large,
the stuffed hippo,
cozy next to Jade's puffed cheek.
I remember my son in his crib,
less than four years ago,
more than ten miles from here,
and I cry inside
for you and Dick and Mandy.
Sleeplessness eats at you
like a rain-swollen river
carving cracks in the earth.
Your longing says Jade is not dying.
We have not talked of that
for a long time,
because we are all dying.
A baby is our joke on the universe,
which always has the final laugh,
or groan, or whimper.

The baby-blue tube
without which she would have died,
scans from Jade's neck
like an alien intelligence.
Her globe eyes roll up like a doll's.
"Soon it will be more difficult."
Euphemisms roll off my tongue
to inflate and fill your dark bedroom.
"At some point…"
"No." Your head shakes, your eyes turn down.
"Please, not the hospital.
Jade stays home
as long as we can do it.
Nurse Martha helps, you help,

everybody helps. Nothing helps."
For both of us I say,
"There will be no resuscitation."
Your black hair nods;
you disguise your eyes.
I want to be sure
we have spoken the words.

8) 5 ½ Months (30 January 1984)

I'm still a young enough doctor
to remember from medical school
the snap, crackle, pop of pulmonary edema,
fluid leaking into dying air sacs.
How small I felt in Bellevue's gothic wards,
listening with my brand-new stethoscope
to the confessions of failing hearts,
the drowning of old lungs.
My teachers were the old, the poor,
the dispossessed.
I haven't heard that sound for years.
Children's hearts rarely fail.
"Sounds like Rice Krispies –
little popping sounds."
"Not bronchitis then, Dr. Jack?"
"No, Pam. It's not bronchitis."

Mandy stands close,
her saucer eyes trying to read mine
and yours and Jade's.
She opens her mouth and points inside.
"Look, Dr. Jack.
A sore in my cheek."
I ask Mandy about her half sister
and her second-grade eyes drift to the floor.
"Jade's going to heaven," Mandy says with surety,

as if she's rehearsed those four words
all her short life.
She looks down at the rainbow of balloons
on her shirt, over her heart.
"Does it hurt, Dr. Jack?
God loves babies, doesn't he?"
I don't know how to answer,
and, in any case, the lump in my throat
would not have allowed my reply.

9) Two days later (1 February 1984)

"Is she…?"
"No, she's much better."
"No more Rice Krispies?"
I will hide my disappointment.
All else will be truth, and trust
between a man from New York City
and a woman on the Canadian border.
"She's so spoiled –
doesn't like to have her nose wiped.
She gets mad."
Delight in her, Pam, as long as you can.
Innocence is rewarded before it is tormented.
You thank me for coming each week –
laying more sandbags against that day.
Another cup of coffee at your polished kitchen table
where faithful friends and relations,
keep vigil alongside your constancy.
"Dick worries me.
He don't say a thing.
I know it'll hit him hard.
I mean, Jade's his only kid and all.
But him and Mandy have got real close."

10) Fog Shrouded Night (11 February 1984)

Fog shrouds the night when Jade dies.
The inverted air is laced with wood smoke.
Her last breath is after midnight,
when there is no time,
when even the living are translucent.
"She didn't hardly have no shoulders at all,"
you tell me as I take off my winter coat.
"But she sure carried a lot of people."
Your doe eyes, all red and swollen,
smile and dance for a moment
as you boast of Jade's supernatural strength.
Where you eat and cook,
family and friends mill about,
sit on the few available chairs,
some with cracked backs.
The men stand, kneading winter toques
in calloused hands.
"Her funeral will be on Valentine's Day.
That seems right to me."
Mandy snores on the big bed
beside Jade's empty crib
and a stuffed hippo.
"I remember sitting here late one night.
Everybody was snoring.
Dick and Mandy and even Jade.
I just listened to their music.
Look at these pictures, Dr. Jack."

Jade's final threads are woven
Into the lush tapestry of her family.
I hold you for a moment knowing
I will carry this broad cloth, forever,
into the foggy night.

Boiling Heart

Michael's chest is scarred over his heart
forever. Boiling water. Six months old.
"Just an accident," you explain, eyes averted,
when I first meet you, Michael's first birthday,
in my clinic on the Canadian border.
I had to report you to the state,
but nothing happened. Just an accident.

You and Michael disappear then reappear.
Now he's three. A fading bruise on Michael's leg,
three inches long, shaped like a stick.
"State lady says he needs shots."

Three boys under five, pregnant again.
I try to understand, but I cannot.
Instead my heart hurts.

Michael's medical chart, in sterile prose,
reports a constant flow of men
in and out of your life.
Errant fathers, and baby boys
you birth with seasonal regularity.
Are you waiting for your girl?
I search for love in your eyes, covert, camouflaged.
You need so much time, but I cannot linger,
my waiting room is packed.

I listen for love in your voice, obscured
by the cacophony of your life and mine.
So much easier to attend the crackles
of a pneumonia I can easily fix.

But there is something else,
shrouded, unless I seek it.
In the dark embrace of your womb,
in this town the railroad left behind,
there must be love or love's mausoleum.
You smack a pack of Marlboros on my desk,
throw down the gauntlet,
and drop onto a hard plastic chair.
I write "??? Abuse?" … the word like acid.

"How many times a day
do you have to spank Michael?"
I'm afraid what you will say.
"Oh," you reply,
as if deciding how much
chopped meat to buy.
"A couple."

And Michael cannot speak.

Failure to Thrive
Pediatric office – Richford, Vermont – 1981

I – Madonna and child

I have seen the wide eyes of famine
on the Canadian border,
where tiny Felicia lies across Maria's lap
staring at me,
dirt lines under her nails.

Maria should be in high school
but Felicia is her third.
Tight black leather pants
and cracked silver nail polish
are powerless
against the black and silver stripes,
like prison bars on Maria's shirt.
No hot water for over a year,
so it has to be all right
for her to smell like the high school
locker room she never changed in.

"Two and a half cans of formula a day?"
I am astounded.
She should be fat and round.
"Failure To Thrive",
I have written it again
after noting her immunization.

Failure surrounds Madonna and child.
For Maria and Felicia
thriving is a fairy tale.
I suggest three weeks in foster care.
"You can visit, stay as long as you like.
I won't take her away.

I promise."
Maria's lips hang thick and parted,
she stares at my words,
begging me silently
to keep it simple.
Or, maybe just gentle.
Her shoulders, eyes, chest, sag,
drag forward, as if gravity
is just too drastic.

Two long days later
Maria and Felicia return
with LeeAnne, her "helper"
who smells of roses and floats
in a full-length purple gown.
LeeAnne digs clay
from the Missisquoi River
and fashions sepia pottery
painted with flowers and birds.

LeeAnne's grace flows over Maria
like a warming robe.
She caresses an invisible baby
at her breast,
her voice like mist.
"There is magic –
a string from you to her.
Maybe we can find the way,
the right way for you."
LeeAnne helps Maria ask the questions
scribbled onto a folded page
from the back pocket
of her leather jeans.

"Will you take her away?"
She cannot look at me.

Stroking her faded denim jacket,
she shifts Felicia from one knee
to the other, and back.

Tiny Felicia pleads with me
through eyes of famine.

II – The Street

The street calls me.
Don't it call you, too?
Through the window,
the one that says
HEALTH CENTER backwards.
The nurse and the potter
tell you it's a mirror
so you can't see nothin'
except you and your kid.
But I know different.
I'm always out there
except when I'm locked in my room.
This ain't what I deserve
for dying in childbirth,
three times.
Ain't that enough love?
You all nod your heads
like puppets at the right time.
We are diseased.
The nurse and the potter
are here to fix us up
in good shape.
Just nod your head,
watch the birdee,
smile,
hand over another baby.
Don't watch the street

though it sucks at you,
pulls you under the door.
My sister kicked me out,
after Justin,
the first time I died.
She spit at me.
"Get out of here.
You give me a bad reputation."

The nurse and the potter
think I don't give a shit.
It's easy for the nurse to care.
She got schoolin'.
The potter lady cares
and puts me on her shelf.
They know what they want.
But nobody knows
how hard it is
to die three times for love.
Nobody.

On the street
my family shares smokes
and Cokes
and good times.
They always love me on the street,
always take me in,
even if Felicia's diaper is soaked
and her bones stick out.
They don't take nothin' from you
on the street.
No nurse, no baby doctor
to spank you till you get it their way.
And you don't have to die for love.

Quality of Mercy – Travis Paul

Travis Paul was born with anencephaly –
failure of his brain to develop –
but a strong heart.
His parents hold him all day
and into that good night,
when his tenacious heart
finally stops at 1:05 a.m.

I am called to pronounce him
in the labour and delivery room
where Travis Paul's father stretches out
on a lounge chair
holding his breathless boy.
Travis Paul's mother, a new mother again,
smiles at me, beatific, sweet,
as if she holds a secret.
Travis Paul's father says proudly,
"We thought he'd only live a few minutes."
He gestures to the wall clock.
"Ten hours. He's like an old man."
Travis Paul's chest is stone silent.
I sit with Travis Paul's parents
and utter inconsequential words.

I feel the boundary,
the precipice we all approach.
Travis Paul has gifted me
a consequential lesson,
how to live with death.

Outside the hospital,
on my way home,
a half moon hangs low in the east,
heavy air sweet with spring.
The moon is smudged on the horizon
by my unanticipated tears.

See This Tooth?

I'm nine years old
and you know what?
Tonight, I'm gonna put this tooth
under my pillow
for the Tooth Fairy.

This year Momma explained,
there is no Santa Claus,
Daddy is the Tooth Fairy
and the Easter Bunny is make-believe.

I nod my head
and say, "I know, I know,"
and she never told me those lies again.

DOCTOR POEMS

Job Corps

I provided medical care for students at Job Corps in Vergennes, Vermont for several years. Job Corps is a residential, federal program that trains eligible young people aged 16 - 24 for meaningful careers (e.g. welding, health care, automotive, digital), and assists them with obtaining employment and high school diplomas. Much of my time at Job Corps involved working with students with emotional challenges, managing their medication and health needs.

Black-Hooded Sweatshirt

A black hooded sweatshirt
covers Tyler's black frizzed hair,
a half-smoked 'Black & Mild'
knuckle-tucked between swollen fingers.
Baggy black ghetto pants.
He can't look me in the eye.
Had we met on the mean streets of Boston,
where he comes from,
I would fear for my wallet,
or maybe my life.
Two tattoos – I've learned to catalogue them.
On his right forearm a flowering crucifix –
"for Grandma."
Over his heart a rugged black face –
"for Grandpa."
Tyler's hands ache in bad weather
from two boxers' fractures,
two right hooks that imploded his metacarpals,
shattered another young man's mandible.
Somehow, by the end of his physical exam
Tyler smiles and we joke
about the tetanus shot he needs.
He's scared.

March 2008

Coy-Boy

Coy-boy, hyper-alert,
bird beak bony face,
buck teeth, stick-skinny,
punched a bathroom stall wall
again and again.
He holds his swollen hand,
like a bird fallen from its nest.
"I don't feel nothin'."
What does he see
when he looks at me?
What does he see
when he looks inside,
into the soup of his soul,
so deceived
by his bi-polar brain.
I think he wants to show me his boo-boo,
how untouched he is by pain,
or maybe just
how far he is from home.

March 2008

Dad Was A Dick

I was born in Wyoming.
(Why are you here?)
Because my Dad was a dick.
Booze and beatings.
Five times she went back to him.
I heard him promise.
(Never again?)
Yeah, never again.
He was so full of shit.
Mom didn't listen to me,
so she got beat up again.
I have a son now. He's two.
His mom won't let me see him
but once a month.
(What's your trade?)
Welding. I'm gonna make it.
If it weren't for my son I wouldn't be here.
(Open your mouth and breathe deeply.
Now breathe normally.
I'm listening to your heart.)

April 2008

God's Son

"God's Son" is tattooed on his neck.
"My first 'tat' – when I was 14."
He squirms, pissed to have to be here
and tell his story yet again.
"My Mom and Dad,
they kicked me out
'cause of this."
He turns his head, arches his neck.
"It's been nine years without a word."
God's Son slouches in the clinic chair.
"I really don't give a shit,"
but his skin squalls at me.
A filigreed crucifix on his right forearm.
"Greed" on his left – an evil clown
scattering playing cards and money.
He shows me blank skin
where he plans to ink the other six deadly sins.

His biggest "tat" is another quandary –
a naked woman with angel wings
arching back, arms thrusting
up his right biceps
into a spiral of stars.
He wants to join the military –
the infantry.
The recruiter told him,
"The naked angel – she's a problem.
Tat clothes on the babe
and you're good to go."

He fingers *"God's Son"* on his neck.
"Can you take this off?"

Love Made Visible

On the right forearm of a farm-boy
from New Hampshire,
in bold mythic typeface.
D Y L A N
No others, only this.
(Who's Dylan?)
"My brother.
It was a tractor what killed him.
Five years ago. He was twelve.
Everything went crazy."
A tear courses his unshaved cheek
like snow-melt through cornfield stubble.
"I miss him every day."
He strokes his right forearm.
"He's with me all the time."

Love made visible.

April 2008

The Boxer

Roberto, small and solid,
sleeps across two chairs in the waiting-room.
I call his name, beckon him to follow.
He squints at my eyes,
his fists all balled up.
My heart squirms with an ancient fear.

He's Puerto Rican and he wants me to know
that he's a boxer.
A damn good boxer.
(How good are you?)
"Golden Gloves - 23 - 0. Lightweight.
My coach was a pro."
(Was?)
I anticipate failure, disappointment.
"Coach got murdered last year – in the hood.
Coach got shot."
I don't know what to say,
so I check boxes on his medical form.
(School?)
"9th grade – left back twice – 2nd and 9th.
I couldn't take no more."

On his right hand – his knock-out fist –
is a rose tattoo – "Maria" across the stem.
He notes my interest and smiles,
Then thrusts his fist at my face.
I flinch – his intention.
"Maria's my mom."

He takes off his shirt so I can listen to his heart.
A shiny, dark wood crucifix
hangs on a wooden bead necklace.
Delicate and hard – like him –
it knocks against my stethoscope.
I hold Jesus away
so I can hear his steady rhythm.
(This is beautiful.)
"From my mom."
(It looks new.)
"Before I come here,
she give it to me."
There are tears in his eyes.
I look away so he can regain his majesty.
I want to hug him.

September 2012

QUANTUM ENTANGLEMENTS

First Draft

Dedicated to those who created the James Webb Space Telescope

Every poem begins as a first draft,
a moment of creation,
a microscopic Big Bang,
a moment that violates
the laws of physics,
a moment to be
a primordial God

The heat of creation cools,
syllables coalesce.
Words spontaneously combust,
joining innumerable stars
to offer navigation,
orientation, pure delight
in our galaxy of possibility,
of love and loss.

The first draft is unique,
unedited, inspired at
the moment of creation.
Turn your telescopes
to this moment and marvel.
You are creating a universe.

Long Trail – Battell Shelter – 12 July 2022

"Spooky" Entanglement

Relationships in our four dimensions
are challenging at best.
We plant seeds in each other,
interact, often at great distance.
Yet, no matter how far,
I carry you in my heart and soul.
We are entangled.
I take this for granted,
it hardly seems strange.
Sometimes it feels "spooky."

In the weird world of quantum physics,
a particle on one side of the universe
simultaneously effects a particle
on the other side of the universe.
A long-distance relationship.
Physicists call it "simultaneity"
and "quantum entanglement."
Einstein had his doubts.
"Spooky action at a distance," he scoffed.
Something has to exceed the speed of light,
and that is forbidden, a civil violation,
three points on your license
and a warning not to reoffend.

And talk about a long-distance relationship.
Lovers connected by something unknown,
something more than banal electrons, photons,
particles and other barely visible
and invisible "spooky" stuff.

What Einstein didn't appreciate,
much less understand,
was love at first sight,
recognition of soul mates
from opposite ends of the universe
and in 11 dimensions.
"Spooky" is another way of saying,
"I love you."

Vermont Long Trail – Cooley Glen Shelter –19 May 2021

False Labor

Hiking The Long Trail to Mount Abe's summit
I am immersed in the thrum of creation,
civilization's cacophony left behind.
The trail is drenched with too much rain,
the forest fecund, adolescent.
An orange salamander obeying vernal dictates
slithers over dead leaves.
Gnarled tree roots hold each other,
consoling, informing,
a lattice stairway across a bog.
After all these years
I am humbled by the immensity.

Walking alone, absent social convention or distraction,
grief wells up as I glimpse my passing away,
my final wilderness adventure,
into trail-less backcountry.
I feel the squeeze of early contractions,
"false" labour, clarion call of the inevitable.
I take comfort in the First Law of Thermodynamics –
energy, essence, my star dust,
can neither be created nor destroyed,
only change form
every birth a Big Bang or a suffused whisper
from which we appear, again and again, obeying,
like the salamander,
immutable laws of gravity and light.

Vermont's Long Trail – Battell Shelter – 17 June 2019

My Indoor Cat

*A meditation inspired by my cat, Lucy. She tests, pokes,
and prods her world in ways that remind me of how I do
the same. Lucy and I, in our own ways, probe the
unreachable and incomprehensible. I draw solace in
camaraderie with Lucy as we try to decipher our
particular place in our particular universe.*

My indoor cat's world is bound
by the walls of my house.
She stares through windows
with astrophysical curiosity
into her unreachable universe.
She studies, with hope eternal, birds at the feeder;
perhaps dreams of escape.
She tests hypotheses, a scientist
probing closets for secrets, toys, food,
another perspective from atop the refrigerator,
or pressed against the ceiling
in the crawl space over kitchen cabinets.
She stares at sunbeams, meditates on motes of dust.
The solar system of her senses is her universe.
She is calm. But in the wild, in the predator's shadow,
she would fear death for an instant,
then walk away, none the worse.

I stare through the same windows at my solar system,
my dot in the universe, and can only conclude
that the hand of God does not extend
beyond my four-dimensional keep,
though physicists, our high priests of cosmology,
weave webs of 11 dimensions made entirely of string.

I wonder about stars I cannot reach.
I stalk the shadow of death,
its meaning, its substance
(it never leaves my restless probing),
no more successful than my cat in the closet.
I test hypotheses with words and, like her,
seek comfort in the crawl space under my quilt
on cold nights, when brittle stars
entice me with their mystery,
mock my deficient explanations,
like dust motes in shafts of light.

Wanted: Muon

Long sought Muon, a fat electron,
wobbled in an intense magnetic field,
violating at least two Thermodynamics Laws
and several lesser misdemeanors.
Before it could be observed,
it fled the scene of the crime,
pursued by heavily armed physicists
carrying standard issue, Standard Model Equations,
with enough firepower to collapse a black hole.
Espionage charges may be brought,
as Muon seems to be entangled
with foreign forces beyond our ken.

The perp has disappeared
after being caught on surveillance cameras
at Fermi National Accelerator Laboratory,
in Batavia, Illinois, by Chris Polly,
a shamus on the case his entire career.
The international search continues.

The vexatious Muon is described as a
fundamental particle (one of 17 at least),
a "fat electron" with a negative attitude, and magnetic
        spin.
Coming of age in the Large Hadron Collider,
Muon is the product of repetitive trauma,
violent collisions with ordinary particles.

Muon is unpredictable and unstable.
It hides out in "empty space,"
(which is not really empty at all. Go figure.)
Muons and other miscreant particles
appear and disappear – exist, and don't exist.

Muons are capable of radioactive decay, firing bursts –
electrons and neutrinos in 2.2 millionths of a second.
A shadowy network of particles
aids and abets Muon, which, before this sighting
was last spotted lurking in 2001
about Brookhaven National Laboratory.
Muon has taunted physicists ever since.
"Muon, you cannot hide forever," said Inspector Polly.
"We have your numbers."

April 2021

Schrödinger's Cat

Erwin Schrödinger, a gentle giant in physics,
considered the intersections –
science, philosophy, ethics and religion.
He sought the Holy Grail –
The Grand Unified Theory of Everything.
(He failed as has every Quantum explorer.)
What do we remember him for?
In a fit of Quantum uncertainty,
while conducting a thought experiment*
without safety goggles,
he concluded that Shady,
the cat he kept in a box,
was alive AND dead.
An atom, he reasoned,
and presumably a cat,
can be in two places at once.
Shady the cat was never the same
after being alive AND dead in a box,
as you might imagine.
(My cat mysteriously disappears
and is often in several places at once,
so this theory does not trouble me.)

Though we seek it relentlessly,
there is no Grand Unified Truth,
only our experience, our relative view,
our daily thought experiments.

2,500 years before Schrödinger,
at the time of the Buddha,
five Indian blind men, wise men,
assessed an elephant and each concluded
with surety, that the gentle giant
was very like a rope,

like a stump, a giant fan, a snake,
or hard and smooth like a spear.
By comparison, Schrödinger's Cat
is only alive and dead.

Both parables suggest the question,
'Pursue an answer
or indulge the mystery'?
Maybe we haven't really come that far,
except that our thought experiments
are more intricate and complex,
our capacity for delusion bottomless.

A crater on the dark side of the moon,
the side we never see, is named "Schrödinger"
to honor his vision of the unseeable.
The Austrian 1,000-schilling banknote,
bears his portrait,

My cat sleeps the restless sleep of the dead,
purring, delighted to be alive.

* **Schrödinger's thought experiment**: place a cat in a
box with a tiny bit of radioactive substance. When the
radioactive substance decays, it triggers a Geiger counter,
which causes a poison or explosion to be released, which
kills the cat. We will not know if this event has occurred
until we open the box. Thus, as long as the box remains
closed, the cat ends up dead and alive at the same time.

(We humans have a tendency to claim absolute truth
based on our limited, subjective experience, even as we
ignore other people's limited, subjective experiences,
which may be equally true. Alive and dead at the same
time.)

When I Say "I Love You"

When I say "I love you,"
the three most complicated words
in every language,
my breath vibrates vocal strings.

Other strings, invisible
but mathematically certain,
vibrate beneath common language,
beneath Newtonian physics,
beneath quarks, beneath particles.
Quantum strings give new meaning
to faith and doubt, to miracles.
The universe may be held together
not by Duct Tape, but by strings.

We live in four dimensions.
String theory requires more;
The four we know and at least seven others
for which we have no words.
We "know" them by mathematics.
Like a chorus, multiple string vibrations
perform the symphony we inhabit.
Strings manifest to our senses
as quarks and particles, planets and galaxies,

According to this arithmetic
"I love you" is a vibrating string.
Who am I? What is this sensation I name love?
Most baffling of all, who are you?
The singing strings reach deep inside.
Our vibrations resonate a duet,
harmony,
        rhythm,
                overtones.

We recognize each other as congruent stardust,
tenderness faster than the speed of light,
connected in a whirling quantum singularity
of particles clumping, of atoms and molecules,
yours, mine, countless others,
careening off the guardrails of our observable world,
catalyzing the unlikely into the inevitable.
I recognize you, with all your quantum fuzziness,
as we exist today, and dream neuron fantasies
of tomorrow, of deep caring for you.
When we touch in this quantum world
there is no barrier. We are liquid
and empty space, mixing essence
in perfect proportion, as if
there really is a point to all this.
Our equations balance and for a moment
the universe is at a still point.
My heart tastes unbearable sweetness.
We are a baffling secret.

Inevitably, things break down.
Grief is another vibrating string,
thus we are gifted with repair,
redemption, lamentation, forgiveness.
Love is messy and intuitive,
gracing us with the quantum uncertainty
of interactions we perceive as
rapture,
       ecstasy,
           and mystery.

If I Tell You My Dreams

will that make them more
or less real?
My hippie right brain tells me
there is only now – no future, no past.
"I love you," present tense.
My severe left brain mandates
a map – a narrative, ghost-written
by cosmologists, astrophysicists,
and other Merlins of the mind.
We have a past and a future.
My left brain explains how,
fundamentally, we are all particles,
stardust packets of order
which defy entropy, for now.
"Groovy," says my right brain,
before breathing in and out again.

I dream of our particles, you and me,
seduced by gravity, clumping together,
collapsing into each other to birth a star,
a planet, a moon, more stardust.
Merlin explains something patently absurd,
but demonstrable –
that no matter how far apart,
even across the universe,
the state of one of my particles
instantaneously entangles with one of yours,
and we are changed.
Einstein called this "spooky action at a distance,"
like a water-filled balloon,
squeeze here, you feel it everywhere,
instantly. Simultaneity.
We are all one.

Some day it will all end for the universe,
though "end" is another left brain speculation.
For now, my dreams are enigmas
for me to assess their more and less reality.
So I wonder, if I tell you my dreams,
will we dream the same dream and be changed,
instantly – spooky action at a distance?
Is this what one – or both – of my brains call love?

World Without Time

Time is nothing more than our conception,
an approximation trying to describe
sensual experience, sentience,
perspective, uncertainty,
our myopic vision, love, ignorance.

Ironically, linear time, our story,
is a side effect of increasing disorder;
entropy, the flow of heat,
that distinguishes past residues,
from future possibilities.

The present is only local –
depending on where we are,
how fast we move.
Clocks tick faster atop Mount Mansfield
than in the Champlain valley.
We don't notice.
This table, almost all empty space
between atomic nuclei,
seems solid, with three spatial dimensions.
We balance heavy plates
on these empty spaces
and eat lunch.

We exist in a gelatinous universe
of constant transformation –
no events, no things, only change,
only process, escalating entropy.
Thus, things cannot satisfy;
we intuit their fraudulence.

I have read that the uncertainty
of quantum approximation
allows for the hand of God,
because nothing is as it seems.
God might indeed play dice
and load the bones
for a particular outcome.
No laws of physics need be violated
by the Almighty merely tinkering
with uncertainty and possibility.

Uncertainty

Time.
Don't get me started.
My watch is analog,
I prefer time's river flow.
Newton would understand,
Einstein would protest.
In our binary world I can choose,
digital ticks, parsing time into quanta,
or the wound spring watch mechanism.
And what about space-time and gravity?
I have been told that I fall
because gravity waves swaddle me
as if I was a massive object,
like Earth or a black hole.
I don't know – it beggars my imagination.

Don't get me wrong.
Except for neutrinos
(speed of light, no electrical charge,
virtually massless, trillions of neutrinos
flowing through me as if I don't exist),
I don't have a problem with particles,
or waves, or gluons that bind us together.
All are adequate creative non-fiction for now.
I just don't like time served up
on a digital platter.
I prefer my time flowing,
downstream, with a pinch of salt.

Toddlers, those bumbling theoretical physicists,
cover their eyes and we cease to exist.
Though incapable of using the toilet,
they seem to know that everything exists only
when observed or interacting.

They bounce from one interaction,
one "quantum leap," to another.
When no one is looking,
they aren't in any precise location at all.

Where or when each particle appears or disappears,
is governed by probability,
the roll of the bones.
Einstein was not a fan.
"It makes no sense," he mumbled.
But we are stuck with it,
challenged to make sense of this
wrinkle from the twinkle of stars.
Is there an agreed upon reality,
independent of interaction and observation?

We need to see, to touch, feel,
indulge our senses when awake.
Is our perceived reality only interactional?
Is there love without it? Do we exist?
The world would be bland indeed
were it not for our collisions,
our bumbling and bumping
conferring identity, dignity,
and affairs of the heart.

When I awaken in the dark dawn,
I look at my analog watch.
I reconnect with my consciousness,
like a toddler, unique and alone
balancing again on life's knife edge.

Left-Handed Universe

Three fundamental interactions –
relationships – govern the star dust
that is you, that is me, that is us.
On a late summer night in 1977,
near Boston, we met.
Electromagnetism and the Strong Force
drew me hard against your polarity.
How did we not spontaneously combust?
We entangled with such quaint notions
as Who are you? Who am I?
In a flash we collided like high speed protons,
indifferent to those around us,
as if they could not exist in our microverse.
Those things that mattered,
and those that didn't matter
cancelled each other out,
like matter annihilating anti-matter,
and only we two remained.
We held each other and kissed for the first time,
two unstable atoms surrendering a bit of ourselves,
breaking down, reassembling,
morphing into a novel element,
and becoming durable again.

On the level of particles,
phenomena occur with either
left-handed or right-handed orientation.
For each left there is a corresponding right.
Hold up a mirror to our uncaring universe,
a left for every right, +1 for every −1, matter for anti-
        matter.
With perfect symmetry they cancel each other
and we do not exist.

But there is a flaw in the universal balance –
without which there would be no Boston kiss,
no Mona Lisa, no Messiah.
Hold up the mirror again,
look more carefully, and this time
a tiny asymmetry, a singular exception—
slightly more left than right,
slightly more matter than anti-matter.
It is as if God dropped a grain of sand
into the stellar machinery
and instead of the void, we exist.

As atoms decay, as worlds fall apart,
they become stable again
and discharge energy.
There is a glimmer of hope
that the imbalance in the cosmic calculation
is something akin to love,
some force conferring meaning.
And we have been trying since then
to figure out how our unlikely world,
with you and me together,
could possibly exist.
We use the word miracle
as a place-holder for understanding.

Beautiful Equations

Dear physicists.
I get it –
your equations are beautiful, elegant,
like illuminated manuscripts
from medieval Old Testaments.
"And God said
let there be light."
Let there be a Big Bang.
Let there be Earth Mother
rising from the shell of a turtle.

Your equations are precise,
a reflection of reality soooo close.
But alas, after millennia of seeking balance
around the cruel equal sign,
they say more about you
than the absolute, God-honest,
dead on balls, no backs, no penny tax,
Grand Unified everything and forever truth.
They beg the question,
what are we here for?

I'm pretty sure that Archimedes
asked himself that question,
but had no doubts about his geometry,
about his lovely proofs that had to be true.
"Give me a place to stand, and a lever long enough,
and I will move the world."

You, Saint Einstein came up with some beauties.
You inserted a fudge factor –
the Cosmological Constant –
to satisfy your equations,
and keep the universe still.

It troubled you deeply.
You called it your greatest mistake.
Now we know (or imagine) you were correct.
The Cosmological Constant is the "best fit"
for Dark Energy, unknown until 1998,
though it seems to be 68% of our universe.

Strange forces entangle us,
others fling us apart.
Einstein's fudge factor was spot-on
though he never knew why.

Do your own math,
move your own world.
You have nothing to lose,
only to sit in the same bathtub
as Archimedes and exclaim "Eureka!"
when you conclude God is a mathematician.
Sadly, another proof will neither dispel doubt,
nor grant a Nobel.
Every creature balances forces,
calculates outcomes.
You can be forgiven for thinking
that every exception proves the rule,
until you realize that every exception
is the longing for love and order –
connection in a chaotic universe,
deaf and blind to our virtuosity, our brilliance.
Be constantly on the lookout
for proofs of triangles,
proofs of love that seem impossible,
another Cosmological Constant,
another beautiful equation.

COVID/Plague

2020 Plague

I sing these trails of my homeland
with elegiac footfalls
over generations of fallen foliage.
A yellow-green striped snake
slithers and crinkles over dried leaves,
then freezes in camouflage.
We consider each other.
Sister Snake neither knows nor cares
about our pandemic plague,
Corona virus – our crown of thorns –
something both living and not
that brings us to our knees.
Climbing above the contagion cloud
that hangs like smog over my village below,
I inhale pristine air and feel
curious camaraderie with Sister Snake
for the fate we share with all creation.

I would feel faint-hearted,
anguished under plague's scythe
were it not for spring's redemption,
soil scent, and crocus courage.
Sister Snake reminds me that death
lurks just over my shoulder
every day, every night, every season.
Sister Snake says, "This is still Eden,
life and death in a *pas de deux*.
I did not tempt you.
The tree of knowledge
still bears succulent fruit."

I pray for Sister Snake, for myself,
for my son, for every creature that rises
from the turning of the earth,
and the fragrance released by death,
inhaled with grief and blessing.

Loosen the bound Earth, free the bulb,
the leek to delight your senses.
Dig with whatever tools you have,
even your bare hands,
to sustain you for one more season.

Chipman Hill – Middlebury, Vermont – April 2020

All Clear!

We have sheltered together,
you and I, for 43 years.
But never like this,
like bears in a den,
like refugees undaunted.
We emerge as butterflies
drying dazzling wings,
anticipating flight again.

We learn, over and over,
that we are neither far removed
nor very different from
fellow creatures great and small,
whose world is fragile and resilient,
who sing their song undaunted,
with courage, beauty, and need.

So, too, our song echoes
from the crevasse of our history,
finding its way like water,
invisibly, inexorably, incredibly,
swelling and cracking seeds of new growth.

Nagasaki/ Middlebury

(9 August 1985 – 40th anniversary of the atomic bombing
of Nagasaki)

My flute mourns
a melody I do not know,
across the Otter Creek
in Middlebury, Vermont – my new home.
Hundreds of candle-boats
float in the creek's current.
Forty years ago
the innocents of Nagasaki
fled to their river
to extinguish the atomic fires
we still douse today.

My first act as a citizen of this Vermont town
is to mourn the souls of Nagasaki,
whose timeless wanderings carry them
to this village where my hope nestles.
I carry their restless flickering in my heart.
My flute weeps consolation and questions.

A Japanese dirge trembles from my lips
as ghosts drift by,
and for a moment
I inhabit grief's deep peace.

INTERMISSION

Anatomicus Anomalous
(or Popliteal Goes the Weasel)

*As a medical student, I spent much of my first year
studying Gross Anatomy. We dissected a human and I
learned all the bones, blood vessels, muscles, ligaments,
tendons, etc. I found the names beautiful, savored their
sound and feel, and composed this poem in appreciation.*

We who work our digitorum to the bone,
We obturators,
Oh Lord, gracilis.

Hail! Infamous infraspinatus.
Reap and sow with glenoid fossa scythe,
Swing subscapularis,
Stand firm tensor fascia lata
In service to sacral obturator externus.

Pineal wizard atop
Atlanto-axial capitellum,
Fix our gaze with sterno-cleidomastoid discipline,
Flex our hallucis longus,
Hold us erector spinae,
Network the interdigitation of
Serratus anterior with obliques,
Lats to glutes, woven through thoraco-lumbar fascia.

Receive each morsel of glottic gift.
Redeem thy communion, pylorus,
Doo-wah, doo-wah, duodenum.
Oh jejunum, to what lengths you go,
Peristalsing past tropical Isles of Langerhans,
Squeezing the sphincter of Oddi for Ichor,
Nector of the Gods
Onto superciliated columnar epithelium,
Cum cecum ca.

Extend our carpi radialis in exaltation.
Suck in the scent of life,
Crista galli, crest of the cock,
Framework for olfaction.
Praise!
Throw wide orbicularis oris,
Orbicularis oculi,
Trigeminal, cranial III, IV and VI.
Carry us, sacred ileum
On our odyssey
Across tibial plateau,
Over pes planus,
The plains of metatarsal
To stand proud at the edge of neo-cortex.

See the Glossary (pp. 111-114 below) for terms used in this poem.

LOVE

An Old Couple

An old couple sits two tables away
eating in silence.
My instinct is to feel sorry for them,
ensconced without a word.
Are they estranged? Did they fight
just before their dinner date?

We have been together for so long,
feeding each other and ourselves,
that I see another possibility,
one so manifest as to be astounding.

The old couple, like you and I,
inhabit an Elysian field
beyond understanding,
where words are superfluous,
even undermining to the duet
we play as we feed each other
with mindful presence, trust,
unspoken affirmation of what is,
what was and what will be,
unfettered by the weight of words,
heavy like anchors
we do not deploy.
We are sailboats catching
veiled wind in our soul-sails.
We skim boundless oceans
seeking acceptance, awareness,
compassion, forgiveness,
feeling beyond words,
communion in the click of his fork,
of her knife on a dinner plate,
in sublime silence.
They leave the café holding hands.

Hummingbird

Hummingbirds' wings beat
50, even 75 times
a second in flight, yet
the frail aerialist hovers,
stillness in motion.
Overnight this petit bundle
of buoyancy and effervescence
enters a sleep-like state of torpor,
8 to 16 hours.
Speed and stillness,
Sleep and frenetic motion.
Unfathomable.

So, too, our life together
hovers and darts,
grows stale and freshens,
torpor and tumult
in metamorphic cycles.
We shed one identity for another,
weep salt tears of loss and grief,
suck nectar from life's bloom,
humming.

Kitchen Hippie

Remember our first kitchen,
in a beat-up Vermont love shack
with a cracked roof
on the Canadian border,
snow-blown State Road 108?
(Or was it a side street
off a side street,
off the Champs Elysées?)
Wind sucked heat from the walls,
chilled my mattress on the floor,
(Indian print bedspread
'60s hippie San Francisco).

We were new,
you hot and spicy,
me cool and dark haired.
You stood at the stove,
wearing only my blue coveralls,
your naked shoulder peeking
through a tear, a rent in time.
You stirred a pan of magical herbs,
added sweet and savory,
a zing of chili,
pepper for resolve,
garlic for courage,
lemon juice for longevity.
You and I, tender and turgid
green scallion shoots,
luminous, not yet sautéed.

It was the old world.
We were fresh and hot,
gazing at each other
like chocolate, in anticipation
of melting.

Maine Coast

Your playful ocean laps
my coast of Maine
boulder-strewn shore.
How often we have sat on this crooked beach,
derelict driftwood, faithful rocks, shifting sand,
hypnotized by the boundary of voluptuary ocean,
the crash of surf caressing a stony shore,
each impossible without the other.

In sleep we float on waves
of flannel sheets and eider down,
the cat curled amongst our legs,
last night's fire smoldering in the stove.
You roll over, a gentle tide
flowing over my body.

Like uncertain toddlers
we fold into each other,
back to belly in our bed,
on our coast of Maine.

The Sacred Is Ordinary

Our backyard gray squirrel
sits on her haunches
between patches of sugar snow
sniffing a dream
of nuts and fruits,
her fragrant fantasy of a mate.

The sacred often feels ordinary.
Cosmologists and astrophysicists,
believe with desperate surety
in 4 fundamental forces of nature,
(gravity, weak force, strong force, electromagnetism).
Not unlike indigenous people's Medicine Wheel,
the four sacred directions,
not unlike Hippocrates' four humours,
blood, phlegm, yellow bile, black bile.

Attachment, like gravity, is holy attraction,
a leap of faith, invisible,
undeniable, incomprehensible.
Compassion and forgiveness,
are the weak and strong forces,
love is electromagnetism.
Physicists seek a Holy Grail,
A Grand Unified Theory of Everything,
one equation binding the four forces.

We catch glimpses of the Grail
in our experience of love.
We perceive the enigma,
hold the question,
give and receive from conception,
entangled in the spark of connection.

You and I met in a magnetic moment,
hewed a nest, birthed our son
from an ordinary improbability.
Even with our sharpest focus,
all is blurred margins, clouded distinctions.
You and I glimpse everything,
the grand unified essence
of this ordinary, sacred moment.

A tufted titmouse drops
a sunflower seed from the feeder.
Our gray squirrel scoops up
another miracle.

Voyage/40
40th Wedding Anniversary

Tugboats ease us from the pier,
from our safe harbor,
past The Statue of Liberty
into uncertain sea lanes
fraught with storms.
Our sturdy craft cuts the ocean
like a plow furrowing loam,
like chevrons of Canadian geese
slicing a blue sky.
We move on, even as we hold on,
graciously bailing the seepage
that leaks into every craft.

Frigate birds announce the shore,
a barely perceptible horizon.
We have sailed an ocean of touching,
an ocean of singing, of music and lyrics,
an ocean of longing
for the harbor, for the voyage.

Gratitude often disguises as ordinary.
But I perceive, in my marrow,
with each heartbeat, our journey's rhythm,
momentous, exceptional,
blessed with grace and good fortune –
and with music,
(Hildegard to Elton John,
Praetorious to Procol Harum,
The Beatles and The Grateful Dead),
the thrumming engine of us together,
bailing the history
that leaks into every generation's vessel.

Journeys begin and journeys end.
Our ship returns to port, to safe harbor,
under our own power,
a blessing, as is the voyage.

.

WILDERNESS

Camel's Hump (The Hump)
Vermont's third-highest mountain

The air and every rivulet is fresh
with too much rain.
Cascades create mud bogs.
At each water crossing I step
cautiously, stone to stone.
The Hump's young ferns and I
contend for even dappled light.

When I could still leap without care,
from rock to rock, over boulder faces
and streams, I strove for competence.
Dreams, yes (oh what dreams!),
sadly tethered by Phobos and Deimos,
mythic gods of fear and terror.
It has been a steep, steady climb.

From the windswept summit,
Earth's existential mass is eclipsed
by a feeling, mystical and revelatory,
unfocused like peripheral vision.
I am grateful for the respite,
for having survived, thrived,
and for my trail mix and water.

At my age, descending the Hump
is more treacherous than ascending.
I bless my climbing as a young buck.
Jealousy needles me when balletic juveniles
leap by, lighting on stones and boulders,
confident of immortality.

Perhaps we'll all meet one day
at the base of the Hump,
in the parking lot, which is filling,
and compare notes.
Maybe we'll have a good laugh.

Burrows Trail to Long Trail – 1 July 2019

Hope

At Minerva Hinchey Shelter
someone left a rock on the table,
gray, rectangular, palm-sized,
painted with the word "Hope" and a daisy.
It's exactly the right size and weight
for the line I throw over a branch
to hang my food sack overnight.

Hope and a daisy in this rock
that I thought was inert.
Half a century ago
Woodstock, another rock –
"An Aquarian Exposition:
3 Days of Peace & Music,"
hope in a world that seemed inert.

In this fragile wilderness
I am sanguine – the air smells auspicious,
the bounty of the Earth envelopes me.
Hope, like the brook beside my tent
springs eternal, singing praise.

"Hope" in this rock weighs
just the right amount for its intent.
It is only incumbent upon me
to throw it high up,
despite all this gravity.

Clarendon Shelter – Long Trail/Appalachian Trail –
August 2019

Instead Of Golf

Instead of golf
I hike these Green Mountains.
Inexorably, my score flounders,
my handicap rises,
but I love it just the same.

Today I don't envy the young ones,
graceful on this rugged trail in particular.
I bless their mileage,
their bagged peaks and wondrous vistas,
their spectacular tales of peril, drama, magic,
of love lost and found.

This is my trail magic –
that I can still climb these mountains,
maneuver among boulders,
up and down rock faces – slower,
but mindful in a novel way.
The full moon wakes me.
I sing to the stars
and dance with my moon shadow.

Swansong (Secret) Shelter on Vermont's Long Trail –
August 2019

To the Trees

The trees got it right,
showing us up
with their test of time,
in which we are but a blip.
We, *Homines sapientes*,
like foals at the starting gate,
exploded into seeming success,
but now we falter.

Trees, who commune
through miles of mycelial networks,
keep their young close,
move with exquisite slow meter,
seeking only sunshine, rain,
and carbon dioxide, waiting
for humans to disappear
into the earth,
like so many fallen leaves.

Remember

Remember – if just for a season –
each fallen leaf, sentient in opulence,
now but memory.
We rise and fall
in our fleeting forest community.
Each season of our lives,
all we know balances
on the knife-edge of history,
of circumstance.
I remember my spring bud bursting,
unfolding and needful,
a slave to the light,
unaware of splendor in my unfurling,

Summer seemed to last forever,
daylight almost constant,
impossible to anticipate the end,
to feel the grace of falling,
flaming from my perch.

We will all lie in state
on the forest floor,
until all colour is gone,
leaving husks and memory,
accommodating the knowledge
that, despite our loveliness,
no amount of grief
will bring us back.

Long Trail – Battell Shelter – October 2020

Sentient Ferns

Sentient ferns listen, in all the ways
I never hear, to the "conversation,"
for want of a better word, or any word at all.
They speak to trees and beetles, to trillium and mayflies.
They speak to me of co-habitation
in our neighborhoods, our niche,
in a diverse and animated biosphere.
This fern is my relative to whom I owe fealty
and respect, not dominion.
We are shepherds, not monarchs.
I have so much to learn from each organism,
each rock, the vibrancy of water,
how to live in balance.
The wild fields, wildflowers, grasses, shrubs,
insects breathing, singing, teaching us
of available bounty, of another way of knowing .

In the garden, Mother Earth loves us fervently,
feeds us, delights and dances with us in all meters
from long and slow melons and eggplants,
to hip-hop carrots poking up and down,
jitterbugging radishes, lightning lettuce.
We turn soil, pour water and hope over seeds.
We are baffled and astounded
by the faithful day-lily,
the sentient fern.

DREAMS

I Dream A World
With homage and thanks to Langston Hughes

Because I dream a world,
my reverie of justice is possible,
though not inevitable.

When snow coats the world,
it bestows a clean sheen,
bleached and milky,
until it dissolves
into soiled ice and crust,
that undermines our footing.
Snow every few days
hoodwinks us into thinking
our world is set right,
clean and white.
We fail to recall the melting
and freezing that trips us up
every time.

America's fatal flaw is
that we are the snow
that never wearies
of camouflaging our blight,
feigning forgetfulness.

Why?

Why do we need "Why?"?
Elaborate answers are unprovable projections,
like antennae, seeking signals of God's podcast
that never come in strong enough,
or long enough,
before scattering into empty space.

Don't waste too much on "Why?"
Buddhists attend to emptiness, impermanence,
suffering, the fog of reality.
Create your own reality.
Too much "Why?" constrains imagination,
the sensation of what is real.
Choose carefully who you are.

Re-create often.
Taste life's spice in each bite,
through each age,
each death and downfall,
each Phoenix rising
to proclaim your grit,
your stubborn refusal
to be betrayed by doubt.
Maybe it's all a dream, so,
why not?

Tuesday's Sunset

I wonder about that Tuesday
65 million years ago,
the day before the meteor
struck, so unlikely.
Did a dinosaur glance at the sky
and wonder at the glow
of just another sunset?
Did a small mammal
blinking at the same sky,
have an inkling of the legacy
about to be conferred upon its lineage?

We dare not take today's sunset for granted,
lest we fail to hold endings and grief
with the same embrace as love.
We have no guarantee,
except that we will die.
It's what we sign off on, the day we are born,
no warranty, no return policy.
Catastrophe in all its disguises
will come, perhaps on a Wednesday,
after the glory of Tuesday's sunset.

NOTES WITH GLOSSARY

Boiling Heart

p. 30. state lady: Vermont Dept. of Children and Families investigator who keeps track of families with a history of abuse, as was the case with this family.

Beautiful Equations

p. 71. "God-honest, dead on balls, no backs, no penny tax, Grand Unified everything and forever truth." These lines are riffs on some street dialogue and children's sing-song ("no backs, no penny tax) and a reference to the "Grand Unified Theory of Everything" that many physicists pursue.

If I tell you my dreams

p. 63 packets of order: the universe tends to disorder (Entropy) with remarkable exceptions – e.g. us, life, music, art, etc. Embedded in Quantum Theory is the notion of tiny packets, Quanta, of order in an inherently disordered universe.

Anatomicus Anomalous
(or Popliteal Goes the Weasel)

pp. 81-82
popliteal: a diamond-shaped space behind the knee joint. It is formed between the muscles in the back of the thigh and leg.
digitorum: fingers and toes.
obturators: two muscles covering the outer pelvis on each side; involved in movements of the thigh and hip.
gracilis: thin muscle of the inner thigh.

infraspinatus: a thick triangular muscle at the back of the shoulder attached to the top of the upper arm bone (humerus) and the shoulder blade (scapula). One of the "rotator cuff" muscles.

glenoid fossa: shallow depression on the shoulder blade (scapula)into which the head of the upper arm bone (humerus) fits.

subscapularis: a large triangular muscle under (sub) the scapula (shoulder blade). It is one of the 4 rotator cuff muscles.

tensor fascia lata: muscle that attaches at the top of your iliotibial (IT) band. It assists motion of the hip.

obturator externus: muscle deep in the pelvis that rotates the leg and stabilizes hip socket.

pineal: pea-sized area of the brain that receives information about light and dark from the environment and produces the hormone melatonin.

atlanto-axial capitellum: First 2 cervical vertebrae, and the anatomical structures connecting them. Provides rotational motion, supports the head, and protects the spinal cord and nerve pathways.

sterno-cleidomastoid: pair of long muscles that connect the sternum, clavicle, and mastoid process of the temporal bone and serve to flex, turn and extend the neck and head.

hallucis longus: flexion of all the joints of the great toe (hallux). From back of the lower leg to the bottom of the foot and great toe.

erector spinae: long strap-like muscles that lie on each side of the vertebral column over the spine. They originate near the sacrum and extend vertically up the length of the back.

serratus anterior: a fan-shaped muscle at the lateral wall of the thorax. Its main part lies deep under the shoulder blade and pectoral muscles.

obliques: two abdominal muscles—the external and internal obliques—from the lower ribs to the pelvis, providing trunk flexion and rotation.

lats: a broad, flat muscle that occupies the majority of the lower back.

glutes: three muscles in each buttock which move the thigh, the largest of which is the *gluteus maximus*.

thoraco-lumbar fascia: a thin membrane throughout most of the back abdomen and neck.

glottic: part of the larynx consisting of the vocal cords and the opening between them.

pylorus: passageway between the stomach into the duodenum (small intestine).

duodenum: hollow tube about 10–15 inches long connecting the stomach to the middle part of the small intestine.

jejunum: middle of the small intestine between the duodenum and ileumabout 8.2 ft long.

islets of langerhans: groups of cells in the pancreas that secrete insulin and glucagon.

sphincter of oddi: a tiny muscle that opens and closes to allow bile and pancreatic juice to flow from the pancreas to the small intestine.

ichor: a thin watery or blood-tinged discharge or fluid taking the place of blood in the veins of the ancient Greek gods.

superciliated columnar epithelium: cells with hair-like projections that move mucus and other substances out of the lungs and move the ovum towards the uterus in the fallopian tubes.

cecum: The cecum connects the small intestine to the colon and is about 2.5 inches long.

carpi radialis: long, superficial muscle of the forearm from elbow to wrist.

crista galli: a small bony plate rising from the nose and containing olfactory bulbs that let us smell.

orbicularis oris: complex of muscles that surround the mouth and lips allowing us to kiss, smile, etc.

orbicularis oculi: sphincter muscle around the upper and lower eyelids allowing us to close the eyelids.

trigeminal, cranial III, IV and VI: the 5th and largest cranial nerve (emerging from the brain), a 3-part nerve that provides facial sensation, chewing and swallowing.

ileum: the last and longest (11.5 feet) section of the small intestine.

tibial: the larger of the two bones of the lower leg.

pes planus: "flat feet," a common foot deformity defined by the loss of the arch of the foot.

metatarsal: long bones in your foot that connect your ankle to your toes.

neo-cortex: the mammalian brain's cerebral cortex involved in higher-order brain functions such as sensory perception, cognition, generation of motor commands, spatial reasoning and language.

ADVANCE COMMENTS

ENTANGLEMENTS
Physics, Love, and Wilderness Dreams

Advance Responses

"Jack Mayer has once again combined a sense of wonder, a deep curiosity. a keen eye, and an almost infinite capacity for empathy and love with the ability to translate those into the 'best words in the best order'. This is a beautiful book about the miracle that each of us represents in this chaotic and somehow ordered universe, especially when we find that special entanglement called love."
> —**Michael Epstein**, Retired Associate Professor of Pediatrics, Harvard Medical School, Founder, www.EpsteinReads.com (Bookmarks) and Chairman of the Board Mary L. Blood Memorial Library, West Windsor, Vermont.

"In this collection of free verse, a physician artfully expresses his being in the world, blending science, wit, and the pang of human experience."
> —**Alan Lightman**, novelist, essayist, physicist, and educator. Professor of the Practice of the Humanities at Massachusetts Institute of Technology (MIT).

"Once again Jack Mayer—a writer I've admired for years—draws close to the white heat of reality. These poems from his personal life and his professional experiences as a doctor compel us to look, to listen. Mayer's poetry makes us, somehow, more alive."
> —**Jay Parini**, D. E. Axinn Professor of English and Creative Writing · Middlebury College, poet and author of *Robert Frost: a Life*, *Benjamin's Crossing*, *The Last Station* and many more.

"From heartbreaking verses evoking his medical practice amidst rural poverty, to the mysterious "spooky action at a distance" entanglement of quantum physics, and on to musings on the covid pandemic, on love, and on wilderness and dreams, Jack Mayer's poems celebrate entanglement in all its aspects—entanglement of doctor and patient, of quantum particles, of long-time lovers, of human and nature, and even entanglement of the body's parts seen as a medical student dissects a cadaver. For all the poems in this remarkable collection, entanglement serves as metaphor for the broader interconnectedness of our world."

—**Rich Wolfson**, Benjamin F. Wissler Professor Emeritus of Physics, Middlebury College.

SOME POETRY AND POETRY COLLECTIONS
Published by Proverse Hong Kong

A Gateway Has Opened, by Liam Blackford. 2021.

Alphabet, by Andrew S. Guthrie. 2015.

Astra and Sebastian, by L.W. Illsley. 2011.

Black Holes Within Us (translation from Macedonian), by Marta Markoska. 2021

Bliss of Bewilderment, by Birgit Bunzel inder. 2017.

The Burning Lake, by Jonathan Locke Hart. 2016.

Celestial Promise, by Hayley Ann Solomon. 2017.

Chasing light, by Patricia Glinton Meicholas. 2013.

China suite and other poems, by Gillian Bickley. 2009.

Entanglements: Physics, love, and wilderness dreams, by Jack Mayer, 2022 (scheduled)

Epochal Reckonings, by J.P. Linstroth. 2020.

For the record and other poems of Hong Kong, by Gillian Bickley. 2003.

Frida Kahlo's cry and other poems, by Laura Solomon. 2015.

Grandfather's Robin, by Gillian Bickley. 2020.

Heart to Heart: Poems, by Patty Ho. 2010.

H/ERO/T/IC BOOK (translation from Macedonian), by Marta Markoska. 2020.

Home, away, elsewhere, by Vaughan Rapatahana. 2011.

Hong Kong Growing Pains, by Jon Ng. 2020.

Immortelle and bhandaaraa poems, by Lelawattee Manoo-Rahming. 2011.

In vitro, by Laura Solomon. 2nd ed. 2014.

Irreverent poems for pretentious people, by Henrik Hoeg. 2016.

The layers between (essays and poems), by Celia Claase. 2015.

Of leaves & ashes, by Patty Ho. 2016.

Life Lines, by Shahilla Shariff. 2011.

Moving house and other poems from Hong Kong, by Gillian Bickley. 2005.

Over the Years: Selected Collected Poems, 1972-2015, by Gillian Bickley. 2017.

Painting the borrowed house: poems, by Kate Rogers. 2008.

Perceptions, by Gillian Bickley. 2012.

Please Stand Back from the Platform Door, by Vishal Nanda. 2021.

Poems from the Wilderness, by Jack Mayer. 2020.

Rain on the pacific coast, by Elbert Siu Ping Lee. 2013.

refrain, by Jason S. Polley. 2010.

Savage Charm, by Ahmed Elbeshlawy. 2019.

Seeking Solace, by Nikhil Parekh, 2022 (scheduled).

Shadow play, by James Norcliffe. 2012.

Shadows in deferment, by Birgit Bunzel Linder. 2013.

Shifting sands, by Deepa Vanjani. 2016.

Sightings: a collection of poetry, with an essay, 'Communicating Poems', by Gillian Bickley. 2007.

Smoked pearl: poems of Hong Kong and beyond, by Akin Jeje (Akinsola Olufemi Jeje). 2010.

Of symbols misused, by Mary-Jane Newton. 2011.

The Hummingbird Sometimes Flies Backwards, by D.J. Hamilton. 2019.

The Year of the Apparitions, by José Manuel Sevilla. 2020.

Twilight Language, by Vinita Agrawal, 2022 (scheduled).

Uncharted Waters, by Paola Caronni, 2021.

Unlocking, by Mary-Jane Newton. March 2014.

Violet, by Carolina Ilica. March 2019.

Wonder, lust & itchy feet, by Sally Dellow. 2011.

POETRY ANTHOLOGIES
Published by Proverse Hong Kong

Mingled voices: the international Proverse Poetry Prize anthology 2016, edited by Gillian and Verner Bickley. 2017.

Mingled voices 2: the international Proverse Poetry Prize anthology 2017, edited by Gillian and Verner Bickley. 2018.

Mingled voices 3: the international Proverse Poetry Prize anthology 2018, edited by Gillian and Verner Bickley. 2019.

Mingled voices 4: the international Proverse Poetry Prize anthology 2019, edited by Gillian and Verner Bickley. 2020.

Mingled voices 5: the international Proverse Poetry Prize anthology 2020, edited by Gillian and Verner Bickley. 2021.

Mingled voices 6: the international Proverse Poetry Prize anthology 2021, edited by Gillian and Verner Bickley. 2022.

Mingled voices 7: the international Proverse Poetry Prize anthology 2022, edited by Gillian and Verner Bickley. 2023.

FIND OUT MORE ABOUT PROVERSE AUTHORS, BOOKS, EVENTS AND LITERARY PRIZES

Web: <https://www.proversepublishing.com>
Our distributor's website:
<https://cup.cuhk.edu.hk/Proversehk>
twitter.com/Proversebooks
www.facebook.com/ProversePress

Request our free E-Newsletter
Send your request to info@proversepublishing.com.

Availability
Available in Hong Kong and world-wide
from our Hong Kong based distributor,
the Chinese University of Hong Kong Press,
The Chinese University of Hong Kong, Shatin, NT,
Hong Kong SAR, China.
See the Proverse page on the CUHKP website:
<https://cup.cuhk.edu.hk/Proversehk>

All titles are available from Proverse Hong Kong,
http://www.proversepublishing.com
Most titles can be ordered online from amazon
(various countries).

Stock-holding retailers
Hong Kong (CUHKP, Bookazine)
England (Ivybridge Bookshop)
Canada (Elizabeth Campbell Books)
Andorra (Llibreria La Puça, La Llibreria).
Also, orders may be made from bookshops
in the UK and elsewhere.

Ebooks
Most of our titles are available also as Ebooks.

Made in the USA
Columbia, SC
18 October 2022

69662070R00067